A TOUCH OF RECOGNITION

ams press
new york

A TOUCH

OF RECOGNITION

Maxine Cassin

ALAN SWALLOW

Library of Congress Cataloging in Publication Data

Cassin, Maxine.
    A touch of recognition.

    Reprint of the 1962 ed. published by A. Swallow, Denver,
in series: New poetry series.
    I. Title.
[PS3505.A852T6   1975]   811'.5'4   72-179825
ISBN 0-404-56025-3
        0-404-56000-8 (SET)

The New Poetry Series

Reprinted by arrangement with
The Swallow Press Inc.
Copyright © 1962 by Maxine Cassin
First AMS edition published in 1975
AMS Press Inc. 56 E. 13th St.
New York, N.Y. 10003

Manufactured in the USA

TO JOE

and

FOR DANNY

when he can read

ACKNOWLEDGMENTS

Some of these poems appeared in the following publications:

Beloit Poetry Journal
The Chicago Review
The Chicago Review Anthology
The Fiddlehead
Hearse
Nine By Three (Hearse Chapbook No. 2)
The New York Herald Tribune
The New York Times
The New Republic
Prairie Schooner
P.S.
Venture
Whetstone

"Benefit Dance" copyright by The University of Chicago Press.

"The Swing," "In Appreciation of Stars," and "The Statue" copyright by The University of Nebraska Press.

"Age 14: Any Color" copyright by Venture Publications.

CONTENTS

III

IV

IN APPRECIATION OF STARS

They bat their sequinned eyelashes
In every quadrant of the sky
And wink at me from years away
As though bewitching were a part
That Nature feels compelled to play.

And since these eyes that look at stars
Emerged in their bewilderment
From some queer cosmic alchemy
And are embroiled within this whole—
To be bewitched shall be their role.

If even chance alone creates
What may be worthy of regard:
A star, a tree, a poem, a face—
Shall these confront for all of time
The blind and windless plains of space?

I

"Now I am terrified at the Earth!
it is that calm and patient,
It grows such sweet things out of
such corruptions."

Whitman

ANIMAL LANGUAGE

Your gesture is in no way schooled,
Untaught, ingenuous this stroke
Falling on me light as smoke,
Yet weightier than tomes of words.
The slight caress, the gentle touch
Of love unforced—from kind to kind—
Inhabits my shrill heart as much
As sudden death or global war.
What made this elemental tongue,
The bond of feeling, tactile speech?
My heart is hidden in your reach.
You find it and begin to talk.

AFTER BLOODSHED

I do not mourn this single death. But more—
I mourn the deaths that must as surely come
As ashes after burning, or as dust
Must follow in the wake of every chore.
Dear God, Dear Enemy, the Law of Dread,
The Alphabet of Anguish and Brute Pain,
Spare us the cruel vision of our dead
Spilled of Love's imponderable stain.

PICNIC

The birds were never very far
And yet they were not very close.
From towers in the sycamore
They scanned our eyes when we arose.

They dove to snatch each crumb we lost.
They flew beyond our widest ken.
We whistled each a song of trust
But they were birds and we were men.

We left our trail of broken glass
And sweet green watermelon rind.
The birds that never came too close
Were never very far behind.

AGE 14: ANY COLOR

Brown girl, tell me, who will you be?—
Twirling your skirt in the summer lamplight.
The children are shouting their games in the night.
Did you outgrow them a moment ago?

In your pause between worlds—how much do you see?
New playmates now beckon with alien games.
You know all their faces but none of their names.
How graceful you are as you turn listlessly.

Afar in the silence, lost to your needs,
Your mother keeps ironing dimity frocks.
Go home, little sister, and comb out your locks.
Wash your face slowly and put off your beads.

THE FEAST

Seldom was a day more chill or trees more bare.
We walked across the fields where small brown birds
Puffed up against the wind to scratch for seed
And you said:

                    "I will bring them bread."
You left my side and winter crossed to me.
A hundred birds flew off the earth at once.
Long silence: till at last your form was held
Smaller than a wren, horizon-still.
It waxed and soon your frost-shined face drew close:

                    "Where are the birds?"
I pointed:

                    "Out in space."
No reproach could fell me more than did
Your shoulders and your small hands letting spill
The sudden snow of white untasted crumbs.

NATURAL PROCESS

My cat beholds a lizard in the vine
And by her cunning and raptorial guile
Does to death one quivering reptile
Simply for dessert and friendly sport.

I fix my eyes upon her avid mouth
Where whiskers and chameleon that were two
Become one monstrous head with double view
Whose conscience battles fiercely with its will.

Ingestion now complete, the cat returns
And settles in the sun to wash her face
As life and death I thought were opposites
Resolve their incompatible assays.

She lies within her summer's noonday haze
And little rainbows rise from a moist lawn.
The low wisteria tentacles bear down
Upon the scene of conquest without hate.

Soon I stroke her gently and she purrs
While in her tract the beady eyes digest
And twitching lizard tails resume their rest
Amid the tireless heaving of earth's bowels.

ON A BOWL BY STEUBEN

Seven pristine gazelles go around in the glass
With the tinkling of wind in their ears.
Opaque are their flanks and their elegant necks
But their sky is transparent as tears

And their breath on the frost-bitten air makes
no haze
As they race on the paths of pure light.
The hound has no scent and no track of their
hoofs
And the hunter is never in sight.

Though the fortunate shepherd may pipe on
and on
And his unravished bride still be true,
The hapless gazelle cannot break from the chase
Of the stalker he never may view.

BENEFIT DANCE

At two dollars a couple
We may contribute to Charlie's fund.
Charlie's left arm has taken leave of Charlie
Swept away on the railroad in the heady
                    November air
With Charlie knowing this departure from
                    himself.
Two feet remain. Will he dance with us
And his transfixed daughters
Intent all night upon the pinkish stump?
The volunteer band salutes a ghostly limb
Spun under the rails, gone far away,
Dancing beyond the tracks—one lonely arm,
Charlie's fingers, wrist, elbow, and gold watch.

THE HOLOCAUST

"The fat is in the fire," intoned the voice.
I saw the flames leap up beyond control
And heard the sizzling of each charring soul,
The panicked face, the desperate lunge for air,
The signalling of fear, the end of choice.

Well, has it ended thus?—while we withstood
The tempter and the temptress and resolved
By absolutes to know ourselves absolved.
The earthen cruet poised above the flame
And tipped to make us vulnerable as wood.

THE MAN

Spare me the story of his genesis.
He is the man of God and does His work.
Let it not perturb you that he failed
Twice at school and once at least at love.
That he had need to prove his mettle
To headmaster or to an upstart girl
Must not distract you from the prime concern

Which is this: that you atone
And walk as humbly as this man does now.

Be not querulous. The microphones
And admen in the rear are merely known as means
And all the bold fanfare sights a single goal

Which is the saving of your dubious soul.

A SUMMER'S REQUEST

If a homely girl whose joys are meager ones
Confides in you that she would like a beer,
Provide it rapidly for her parched bones
Whose thirsts are even deeper than her fear.

Since she is weary and her pleasures rare
Who seeks to drown the constant taste of brine,
Deprive her of no simple lust tonight
For golden ale that foams in its chilled stein.

Therefore, little one, your wish commands.
Clap hands and bring the quenching cup of cheer
For a lady with straight hair and lonely eyes
Who says in earnest she would like a beer.

ANNALS

This was the year of the blackbird.
That was the year of the swallow.
Time is a bird on the wing.
Today is an owl in a hollow.

Tomorrow will be for a robin.
Yesterday's only a lark.
But the evenings of Spring are to me
Three nightingales singing at dark.

II

"Here the frailest leaves of me, and
  yet my strongest lasting.
Here I shade and hide my thoughts—
  I myself do not expose them
And yet they expose me more than all
  my other poems."

                              Whitman

THE SWING

Chained by bonds of love,
It moves within limits,
Rising and falling on air,
A child's arms above it

Hugging with steadfast ache
The link on which depends
Her safe suspension through a time
Of flying innocence.

Hooks convey delight.
Down streams laughter in braids;
Heavenward soars the heart
Only for today.

When she goes, the prisoner
Motionless under stars
Dreams no rare escape
From the way things are.

THE STATUE

Stonewall on his pedestal
Is visited by birds,
Swallows on his epaulettes
Incapable of words.
Sun and wren are merciless
But evening doves are kind.
They gather underneath his steed
To mutter without mind.
And when the night falls on the square
They leave him all alone
To gaze on the cathedral wall
With moonstruck eyes of stone.

AS I WAS DUSTING

Waxing eloquent,
From the mantel spoke the candle:

"I stand as you require.
 When light fails elsewhere
 I am your slender hope.
 As you fondle me, remember
 Your childhood's darkest hour.
 In its storms I surrendered
 Myself to scathing fire.
 While molten teardrops hardened
 I made light of sacrifice."

THE COMFORT

How empty is her womb. A morning sky
Has chilled her with its grey and vacant stare.
The breeding cat crawls up into her lap
And curls its claws upon the softness there

Until it lies upon her in a sleep.
The kittens stir a little. She is warmed.
The life outside of her, its throbbing weight,
Seems real beneath her heart and she is calmed.

IN THE GARDEN

The slightest of the moths could bear him upward.
Simply a cloudless sulphur was enough.
And a swallowtail! He soared aloft on breath
Till a fluttering of wings caught in his throat.

Excess of summer? Which conjecture heals?
He stands among the monarchs in the sun,
Boulder-still. The flapping shadows brush
Against the petals of a dying rose.

ETUDE FROM THE BAYOU COUNTRY

These oaks have stood a century, perhaps,
Forgiving the parasitic moss,
Dangling it unconcerned from sturdy branches—
Saying: the strong abide the clinging.

But in the swamps the strangled forms, moss-draped,
Tell us differently: how air grew thin
And sunlight lost, how the grey nooses
Tightened without mercy.

The giants, picturesque in parks,
Wave their misty banners and scoff at this,
The curly locks of moss flung round their necks.—
How could she stunt? How could she ever kill?

BURNING BRIGHT

The extravagance of cats beware.
Though Pater lost his page of Baudelaire
He later kissed his Persian on the stair.

Well! One forgives so much for loveliness.
Hector's dead but Helen is no less
Desired for a feline wantonness.

Loyal is the dog, subservient.
Throw out a bone and he will gnaw, content.
The liver and the heart were always meant

For those who show us gratitude by claws,
Who are quite unaccountable because
Fierce love exempts their kind from human laws.

WORK OF ART

She was a frieze on the temple front,
Half cut away from stone,
Not realized enough to caress,
Her backside anchored to parental bone.

And her creator chiseled her like this,
Hoping she could never turn around
To know the faceless granite where emerges
The eyes that see, the mouth that makes a sound.

SUMMER STORM

Light are the boughs in the wind,
In the drought, in the air
Till the shower that breaks the spell
Bends them down with care—
For the seed, for the life that needs
More than wind, more than sun.
They are laden with rainfall now,
All their frolicking done.
And this weight which their heaven sends
May they safely bear—
For a branch may bow and break
Before it is fair.

MOTHER AND CHILD

Lifting you down from the edge of a chair,
My musings begin—
Even here in the simple ministry
Of drying a chin.

Holding you a moment off the ground,
Your arms about me,
I force myself to bring you back to earth
And let you go free.

WHOSE HOME?

Now if the moth abides with me,
Is mine a house of moths?
My child, who is a child of three,
Gave me his small thoughts.
And I have kept them in my head
Much longer than he knew.
Do the vermin in your walls
Really live with you?
Do the microbes in your breath
Pray each time you pray?
Do I reside in someone's mind
And quickly fly away?

THE BOYS

You might say you met each other in a way—
Although it was before you saw the day.

I carried you beneath my heart, and she
Was full with him, this bursting lad of three.

Now you play together in the light
With words and shouting—who were once so quiet.

You smile and move inside a wider world
With every perfect limb at last uncurled.

Tell them now: "Here is a friend of mine
With whom I shared a separate lonely time.

"We could not see each other in those weeks;
Now I hear him clearly when he speaks.

"We could not touch. Today I feel his hand
A little wet and gritty with the sand.

"We have much darkness and so little space
For learning love before we're face to face."

IN PREPARATION FOR ROSH HASHONAH

As the High Holidays draw near at summer's end,
Before the New Year's solemn opening,
The sexton has a laundress in to wash
The prayer shawls and do the ironing.

Lest scrolls may mould, he suns them one by one—
Unrolling books of Moses to the light.
Leviticus grows warmer to the touch;
The fire in the bush burns hot and bright.

An empty Ark envisioned troubles him.
He piles the Torahs underneath his chin,
And like young babes in velvet swaddling robes
They rest within his arms as they go in.

PLANETARIUM

Though stars are apertures of light
The eye does not know otherwise
And music from projected spheres
Can artfully deceive the ears.
Five senses are with ease beguiled
But not the sense that clocks our days.
When suns abandon us too fast
We are aware how light should last
And can infer from here a door
Into the world beneath the sky
Where no one flicks a dipper off
Or sees unscheduled moons go by.

GESTURE

The nurse at the bedside rewinds the clock—
2:30 among tall stemmed gladioli.
The heart falters, then begins again
Its rhythmical tick-tock.

She who coiled the mainspring tight
Departs until tomorrow,
Having assured herself that time
Will beat for you through the long night.

WINTER

In this ruthless light
Striking us through branches without leaves
We look up, squinty-eyed, into a clear
        December sky.

No clouds are spun out now like cotton candy.
No shapes are here to bear our dreams,
Profiles with beards to ride enchanted ships,
No, not one form that steers—
Only the blightless slate
Whereon a word may watch
Its own beginning as it disappears
And contrails fade from heaven with no trace
As a leaf, the last of all, falls into space.

III

"Vitae summa brevis spem nos vetat incohare longam."

Horace

"If you had said one false word to-night I'd have
really gone mad."

Henry Miller

FOR YOU, A READER

I should like to be thought of as thinking.
It is a harmless posture you allow me.
Cogitas, ergo sum. Thus I exist
To your mind quite necessarily

As to my own. Therefore we are
The result of our imagining
Conjectured into life beyond facade
Irrefutably in common feeling.

FOR THE PROCRASTINATING SELF

Is it too late to make a beginning
As I should have done?
For I have never properly begun,
Not truly, that is, until
Now, and Now is the only time
That what begins begins for anyone.

Are there really fewer tomorrows
For seeing through a plan
Than there were when I almost began
But didn't? Had I insurance Then
That I could finish—anymore than Now?
And Now may be the only time I can.

THE GUEST

The rapping at my door at midnight
Was a black hound scratching fleas.
In the moment before illumination
I invented mysteries.

What do you do then, when the stars
              are veiled
And pounding wakes the sudden shade
You thought you had dispelled?

Hope admits the ghost the mind must
              lay to rest—
The ancient bones our dog had witlessly
              enfleshed.

THE OVERSENSITIZED

You trod upon my fingertip;
I sucked the air from pain.
How strange I never felt it
When you bored into my brain.

And when our beings barely twined
I swooned with such delight,
I made an anti-climax of
The rest of every night.

When we were formed the flaw inhered
In those so keenly set,
We never fend the actual blow
But stagger from the threat.

Before we know a truth at all
We have it preconceived
And every death that comes to us
Has been already grieved.

THE PRICE OF SONG

"The earth is moved from its position by the weight of a tiny bird resting upon it."

Leonardo da Vinci

Leonardo, yes,
Death was your milder rage.
Slaughter stirred you less
Than songbirds in a cage.
You paid the price of freedom
To let a finch digress.

What of the unplucked hen
Lying stiff and cold?
Had you no sorrow then,
No quick display of gold,
To spare her for awhile
From the wrench of men?

As ever, all great Art
Has scorn for sentiment
And gives its utmost heart
To Beauty's instrument
While Death claims all the rest
Who cackle in the mart.

The colossal vacuum Time
Into which have run
The minutes and the days,
The scorn and gentle praise—
It sucks and yet it sucks.
The heart's blood flows away,
The fleshy parts decay
Till shrinking bones remain
Dissolving into lime.

This ache of Nothingness
Creates but to devour,
Feeding its maw with us
Until some unknown hour,
Erupting from its greed,
It spews the night with dust.

And dust will coalesce
And man will rise from dust
To write of this again.
Betrayed by his own trust
And lack of memory
He even finds it just!

FALLOUT

Out of the slime we rose
And brought with us a nose
To scent what might attack
And hurl a creature back.
And yet no nostril knows
The putrescence which flows
Out of the mushroom cloud
That made the nations proud.
And not an eye can tell—
Our sight which serves us well
To recognize a foe
Perceives no deathly glow—
While all around us grows
A vast miasmic rose.

LOVERS' DECLARATION AT NUCLEAR
TESTING SITE

It is not upon this blazing ground we stand
To search each other's hearts for verities.
Ours is an earnest business in some land
Of gentleness and small amenities.

If Nature's bond is broken on our shores,
We gasp to learn the great ferocity
That keeps together even tiny spores
And gives each particle identity.

We would be slow to tamper with such Will,
Flagrant as it is. Let us intend
The union of parts—whereof there comes no ill
And luckily some goodness in the end.

But, as the facts will have it, atoms fuse
To set the sun exploding into light.
Now man may bring down darkness if he choose
As with our cleaving we solicit night.

DEVIL'S IVY

It took us by surprise in the unwinding chore
Which we began upon its withering.
This vine that climbed a distance toward the sun
With every inch of its unthwarted will
Depended on a slim margin of stem,
One bloodless artery into the soil—

Too slight a bond for all its leafy weight.
And yet it thrived for years, deriving here
As much earth sustenance as was required
To build its line in time, a certain growth.
Uncoiling it is not irreverent;
We celebrate the paltry source of things—

And think it far, far better to imagine
Beginnings that are frail or trivial.
We must answer for a great deal more, of course,
When oaks shrink down to acorns as they last.

IV

"I swear, gentlemen, that to be
too conscious is an illness—
a real out-and-out illness."

Dostoievsky

TRIO

Lorenzo, our tiger diminished,
Is almost falling asleep.
There are two of us now in the lamplight
Watching his eyes glaze and close.

Acquiesce? Let the nightflood come in?—
A cool tide over our wills.
No, let us as sentries remain
Guarding what dreams may disclose.

But the white wine of silence is strong.
Now you doze. I am clinging alone
To my vestige of mind in the dark,
Holding words on the tip of my tongue.

COSMIC CHANNEL

Now what will entertain me at this hour?—
After the ultimate news, the final prayer,
When every station abdicates its power
And each round dial leaks silence through the air.

A walk in the dark to view the gibbous moon?
Also a blank! its pale and pock-marked screen.
Does nowhere a celestial buffoon
Let his vast absurdity be seen?

Only the star, the coldly distant one,
Transmits a world that happened long ago.
The brilliance of an ancient, perished sun
Provides the universe with its late show.

A PLEA FOR STAYING UP LATE

The vise now closes on a nodding brain
Darkening the vision; body lies
Flaccid as a rabbit newly slain.

Call to it now: Arise! and let us look
First at each other, second at the sky,
And third into one true and lofty book.

Hang on, hang on awhile and keep awake
For pain is a kind of knowing, though unkind,
And mindlessness the last profound mistake.

STAR-GAZER

We watch a sun that is not there,
Enlightened well enough to know
The source of our attention cooled
And faded out some time ago.

How much deception can we bear?
The twinkling of an eye long dead
Binds us in this spell of night—
To a sense-illusion wed.

MORPHEUS

I have outdistanced him yet now admit
That I would be relieved if overtaken
But see this god! he will deny me sleep
As before he had refused to let me waken.

Between too much awareness and then none
I would discover that cool resting place
Where Time, a tardy hare, starts up to find
The tortoise has slipped by to win the race.

LONG DISTANCE

Operator, I have placed a call.
Let the phone ring a long time,
I must be convinced
That no one is at home—
That tonight, except for
The starry switchboard,
The whole blamed world is out.
Nevertheless, I will hold the line
While the pulsing bell from far away
Lulls me until I feel
An answer is irrelevant.

THE LOGICIAN

Since it is not within my power
  (easy enough to acknowledge)
it must be in another's power
  (not difficult to anthropomorphize)
therefore I conclude that I may pray.

I am supplicant consequently
(a little bit harder to kneel)
and what shapes me, sustains me,
offers the necessary ear.

And that is all I can assume,
the postulate of a listener—
when the waves of sound are gathered
into words at the edge of darkness.

THE REFRIGERATOR

Thus I began the contemplation of the dark
as it came to me in the cool taut night
when the door clicked shut and the light
                    went out
cold bottles stood upright and sometimes
                    froze.

But I never knew them as they are in their
                    inviolate dream.
Only at morning the chill fruit jar,
the pale milk ghost, the stubby cream
touched me waking hungrily.

THE AWAKENING

Haul, haul, morning maid
With your strong lithe arms.
From the swirling waters raise me up
Spilling over dreams.

I am clear now, clear in soul
From the deep springs underground.
You can pour me for ablution
On each manmade wound.

HONESTY

At the bottom of my cup
The shape of soggy leaf
Suggests a sudden grief.
I try to tip it up
And rearrange perchance
The deadly happenstance,
But conscience makes me stop.
I drink the final drop
And hand my cup and plate
Into the hands of fate.